What's Making You Angry?

10 Steps to Transforming Anger
So Everyone Wins

*A presentation of Nonviolent
Communication™ ideas and their use by*

Shari Klein and Neill Gibson

PuddleDancer
PRESS

For additional information:

Center for Nonviolent Communication
5600 San Francisco Rd. NE Suite A, Albuquerque, NM 87109
Ph: 505-244-4041 • Fax: 505-247-0414 • Email: cnvc@CNVC.org • Website: www.CNVC.org

ISBN: 978-1-892005-13-7

Contents

What's Making You *Angry?*

Introduction

When we are angry, three things are happening: 1) We are upset because we are not getting our needs met; 2) We are blaming someone or something else for not getting what we want; 3) We are about to speak or act in such a way that will almost guarantee we will not get what we need, or that we will later regret.

When we are angry, we focus almost completely on what we *don't* want, and our thinking is caught up in images of the wrongness of others that are involved. We have lost sight of what we really *do* want and need.

Using the steps below you will learn how to change this pattern and connect with the life-serving purpose of anger. You will discover where anger comes from and learn how to express it in ways that meet both your needs and the needs of others. Use these steps to re-focus your attention during an angry conflict and learn to create outcomes that are satisfying for everyone involved.

STEP 1

Think of Anger as a Red Light on Your Dashboard

Anger acts like a warning light on your car's dashboard–if you attend to it promptly you're more likely to get where you want to go. Remember, when dealing with anger the goal is not just to "turn off the red light." Anger can be a wonderful wake-up call to help you understand what you need and what you value. Like warning lights and gauges, your emotions and the physical sensations in your body are there to help you understand which of *your needs* are being met or are not being met.

So, when tempers flare or violence looms, it helps to remember that you can make life enjoyable for yourself and others if you focus your attention on what you need, and put aside any ideas of the other as "wrong" or images of them as the "enemy." Make it your goal to attend to your underlying needs and to aim for a resolution so satisfying that everyone involved has their needs met also.

STEP 2

Look Clearly at What Happened

Have you ever asked a person what they are angry about? Most likely, they told you that someone said or did something wrong. One example might be an executive saying, "He's unprofessional! He ruined the presentation! He was disrespectful to everyone in the meeting!" Such statements say very little about *what really happened.* In this step you want to be like a detective—you want "just the facts." Notice the difference in the quality of information between the previous statements and the following: The executive might have said, "He arrived twenty minutes later than the scheduled start time, and brought coffee-stained handouts."

In this step you take a clear look at *what* you are reacting to. When you can objectively describe what happened you are more likely to be clear about what you need. Other people are less likely to respond defensively because they can more easily agree with what you've said. So, the second step in dealing with a charged situation is to be able to state a clear observation of the situation itself.

Statements from an angry spouse, such as "You insulted me," "You're a control freak," or "You're always trying to manipulate me," imply wrongness, but they *don't* describe what actually happened. With the aim of making a clear observation, you ask yourself, "What would a video camera have recorded?" With this perspective you might be able to describe the situation very differently. "I heard you say I'm a lazy slob." "You said you wouldn't go out with me unless I wore the red dress." "You said I always wear clothes that are out of style." Once you can clearly describe *what* you are reacting to, free of your interpretation or evaluation of it, other people are less likely to be defensive when they hear it.

STEP 3

Take Responsibility

Anger is also a signal that you've been distracted by judgmental or punitive thinking, and that some precious need of yours is being ignored. Use your anger to remind yourself to stop, look under your hood and into your heart to find out what needs attention.

When your car's water temperature gauge is in the red, your engine's need for cooling is not being met. When your car's battery warning light is off, your charging system is doing fine. Like these indicators, your emotions and the physical sensations in your body are very powerful and accurate indicators of the conditions under your personal hood. They are designed to tell you very quickly and clearly, in each moment, which of your needs are—or are not—being met.

Keep in mind that other peoples' actions can never "make" you feel any certain way. Feelings are *your* warning indicators. Your feelings always result from whether or not your needs are being met. Anger results from focusing your attention on what another person "should" or "shouldn't" do and judging them as "wrong" or "bad." As your attention shifts to identifying which of your needs aren't being satisfied in a situation, your feelings will shift also. When you discover that you didn't receive treatment that met your need for respect, you might feel hurt, scared, or disappointed, but without "should" thinking and judgments of others as "wrong" you won't feel angry.

When your feelings have served their purpose—when your attention is fully focused on your needs and values—then anger melts away. This transformation is not the same as repression, and it's not the same as "calming down." The emotions you feel when you are in touch with your needs may be intense and very painful, but they will be *different* emotions than anger.

"Name the Blame" and Get
Clear About What You Feel

In our culture most of us have been trained to ignore our own wants and to discount our needs. We've been called selfish for "wanting," and "needy" when we voice our deepest yearnings. But the fact is that *everyone* has needs, all the time. Every human being needs respect. Everyone needs nourishment, harmony, self-expression, and love (to name a few basic human needs). The only humans who don't have needs are dead.

When you're angry you are likely to have "blame thinking" going on in your head. Inside of "blame thinking" you have emotions, and these are caused by unmet needs. When you can get conscious of your "blame statement" you can begin to explore your feelings and use these feelings to get clear about which of your needs are going unmet.

For example, if your blame statement was, "She's always insulting me," what emotion or body sense would you feel? Would you feel tense, scared, sad, anxious, or confused? Naming our feelings is not as easy as it sounds! As a society we are trained to mix our evaluation with our feelings and this is what gives rise to "blame statements" in the first place. Separating your feelings from your judgment of others is an important part of getting clear about your needs and moving into action to get them met. You can use the feelings inventory in chapter four of Dr. Marshall B. Rosenberg's book, *Nonviolent Communication: A Language of Compassion* (PuddleDancer Press, 1999) to develop your *vocabulary of feelings* and learn how these feelings relate to your needs (see Basic Feelings list at the back of this booklet).

STEP 5

Determine Your Needs

"Wait a minute, my reliability warning light is on!" The executive who thought the employee "ruined the presentation" remembered that his anger was just a warning. When he looked underneath his anger, translated his judgments and discovered his underlying needs, he realized that he values reliability, integrity, and trust very highly. Focusing on these needs brought a shift in the executive's state of mind. His anger dissolved. Instead, once in touch with these unmet needs, the executive felt *worry* and a pang of *disappointment.*

Even the harshest labels like "psychopath" are just veiled expressions of unmet needs. When a person calls someone a psychopath, it's a tragic expression of their unmet needs, possibly for predictability, trust, or safety. It's tragic because the very *act* of calling someone a psychopath almost guarantees that the underlying needs will continue to go undiscovered, unexpressed, and unmet.

The beauty of being able to correctly interpret your feelings as warning signals is that, once you discover what you need, you are back in a powerful position to act toward getting your need met! You can use the human needs inventory in chapter five of *Nonviolent Communication* to develop your *vocabulary of needs.*

Having named your need, spend some time really noticing how important that need is to you, how you yearn for it, and how much more satisfying life is when that need is satisfied.

Practicing Nonviolent Communication guides us to reframe the way we listen to others and express ourselves by focusing our consciousness on four areas: what we observe, feel, and need, and what we can request to enrich our lives. In this context the word "need" defines those basic human needs we all share. At the end of this booklet is an abbreviated list of what Nonviolent Communication would define as basic human needs.

As we learn to focus our attention on meeting these needs we begin to connect at that place within us where we are all essentially the same. This helps us cultivate deep listening, respect, and empathy, which engender a mutual desire to give from the heart, and allow our natural compassion to flourish.

 ## You're Half Way There!

In the previous steps you explored *how you are*. In Step 2, you took a more accurate look at what the other person did. In Step 3, you took responsibility for your feelings, and in Step 4, you took ownership of your thinking and began to look underneath at your natural feelings and needs. You chose to use your thinking powerfully, as a way to clarify what you *value*. In Step 5, you experienced a fuller sense of self because you're in touch with your needs.

In the following steps you will explore *who can do what* so everyone's needs will be met. With Step 6, you begin to envision *actions* that are in harmony with meeting those needs.

STEP 6

Find the "Do" Behind the "Don't"

When people are angry, they often focus on the behavior that they want the other person to stop. This is similar to wanting your car to stop overheating. You can want your car to stop overheating but you're stuck with a car that overheats until you identify what needs to be fixed and take the actions needed to fix it.

The executive in the previous example may identify that he needs greater trust and reliability when it comes to presentations being made on time and with materials he enjoys using. If he has been trained the way most of us have, he may be tempted to think he wants to tell the other person, "Don't show up late and don't bring coffee-stained handouts." The problem is that the person may not show up at all rather than being late, or show up without handouts rather than with soiled ones.

He is much more likely to get his needs met if he can come to an agreement around a "positive" request that states clearly what actions would meet his needs. For example, "Would you agree to call me 30 minutes before the meeting so I know you will be on time, and put the handouts in a protective envelope as soon as they are copied?" Place your focus on what you *do want*, not on what you *don't want*.

Think of a Clear Action Request

Earlier, you saw that angry people think they're angry because other people *made* them angry. Now you harness the power to undo this misconception and focus on the *power* you and others have—the power to deliberately make life more wonderful through the use of a "present tense" request.

"I want you to be reliable" is not a clear and doable request. In this step, the idea is to envision the other person doing or saying something *right now* that is in harmony with your desire and likely to meet your need. Ask yourself, "Right now, what could the other person say or do to honor my needs?"

For instance, a man passed over for a long-expected promotion was keenly aware of his unmet needs for recognition and respect. He was already clear about how to say what had happened, his feelings about it, and his needs. Only then did he consider making a very clear "positive action" request. He decided that the following would be a good beginning request for the dialogue he wanted to have with his boss: "Would you review at least two projects with me that I completed this year, and that you believe improved the company's market position?"

The man realized that his request was a "future request" and to really stay connected with his boss he wanted to make a "present action" request. To do this the man asked himself what action his boss could take in the moment he made his request.

He figured out two requests that his boss could respond to right now. The first was starting with, "Would you agree to . . . " This creates an agreement in this moment to do something in the future. It is something the other person can respond to immediately. He also added, " . . . within the next week." This request creates a definite time period during which the agreed-upon action will take place. Now the complete request is positive in action language and in time. "Would you agree to review with me, within the next week, at least two projects that I completed this year, and that you believe improved the company's market position?"

STEP 8

Name Their Feelings and Needs

Just like coins, every situation has at least two sides. If you really want to reliably meet your own needs, it is important to make sure that the other person's needs are met as well. This step is about demonstrating your understanding that your needs can never be fully met at someone else's expense. It is about shining the light of awareness on your own feelings, needs, and requests, and shining it on people in your life as well.

Use steps 2 through 7 to guess in your mind what the other person is experiencing. The essential element is to guess without worrying about guessing accurately. This is your best attempt to imagine what the other person desires, what the other person needs when they are acting as they do.

Remember, you haven't started talking yet. You're thinking hard, but you haven't spoken to the other person yet.

So guess at their feelings. Translate the statement, "He's compulsive" into what you imagine the other person *does want.* For example, maybe they crave beauty and order (and that's why they're after you to pick up the dirty socks on the floor), or maybe they are yearning to be nurtured, cared for, or loved (and that's why they complain about you spending time with your friends). At this point, even though you are not talking to the other person yet, you are seeing the person differently. You are replacing your "enemy" image of the other person with a vision of something beautiful and sweet—the vision of a human being with needs, who seeks to make life more enjoyable by satisfying those needs.

STEP 9

Decide Whose Need You Will
Talk About First

Think big. Enjoy imagining that everybody's needs will be understood and honored, that no one will "win" at someone else's expense. The process is complete only after both people have been heard and understood and walk away satisfied. You're not done if only one person has been heard and understood.

Only one person, however, can be heard *at a time*, so ask yourself several questions to determine who will speak first and who will listen first. Do you want to express how you are and invite the other person's understanding? Or do you want to extend your understanding to the other person first? Who is in the greatest distress? Who has the greatest clarity? Consider what happens when the person with greater clarity chooses to focus their attention first on hearing the feelings and needs of the person in greatest distress. Being heard in this way, the other person will most likely experience relief and clarity, and be more willing to consider your needs.

Either way, you are the one to focus the light of awareness during the conversation. You will be the one who will focus on *feelings*, *needs*, and *values*, and determine whose needs to explore first. If you choose to *express*, you'll be revealing your feelings, needs, and requests, which you identified earlier. If you choose to *receive*, you'll invite the other person to reveal their feelings, needs, and requests, which you guessed at in the previous step.

STEP 10

Now Start Talking

Ask yourself the following questions before you begin talking: Are you clear about what you're reacting to? Are you in touch with your feelings and needs? Do you have a hunch about the other person's feelings, needs, and values? Do you know what you want to happen next? Okay, *now's* the time to talk! Here are some suggestions about what to say (and what not to say).

First, don't say anything from Step 3. This is the blameful thinking that fueled the anger in the first place. Instead, stick to Step 2 and state a clear observation ("I have been thinking about how you spend three nights a week with your friends."). Then jump to Step 4 and be open about how you are feeling. Remember to choose a feeling that comes from the heart or a body sensation, like "I feel lonely and sad." Watch out if you start by saying, "I feel *that*..." or "I feel *like you*..." Remind yourself that what is likely to follow is analyzing or blaming, and that you are unlikely to get what you want by speaking this way. *Remember*: express emotions and body sensations, not analysis or blame.

Once you've named the feeling that replaced your anger when you got in touch with your needs, name your needs out loud ("I realize I need more companionship than I'm getting."). Then make a request that invites a response that will make life more fulfilling *right now* ("Would you be willing to agree to spend every Tuesday and Saturday evening with me?").

The other person will also want understanding for their needs. But chances are that they won't have done all the internal work you just did. They will probably go straight to Step 3.

They may be saying something out loud, like "You're so selfish—it's always about you, isn't it?" They're just the blameful sorts of things you've just refrained from saying to them! That's okay. You can handle it. Choose to empathically receive whatever they say. Move your attention to *their* feelings and needs. Guess what action they might like you to take. "So are you worried (feeling) about consideration for your needs (need) and want to know that I am willing to consider them as well (action)?"

Telling a person that you hear what they want *is not* the same as agreeing to do it. By hearing what they want, you make sure you understand clearly so you can *let them know how you feel* about doing it. When you demonstrate that you really understand what they feel and need, you will be amazed how quickly they will trust that their needs are important to you, and as a result will be open to considering your needs in return. They are also likely to be more receptive to various strategies for meeting their needs.

So, Let's Recap

In steps one through three you learned new ways of understanding and relating to your feelings of anger.

In **STEP 1** you learned that anger is a valuable warning signal that tells you to stop and look under your "emotional hood" at your feelings and needs, and to begin to look for outcomes that would make life more satisfying.

In **STEP 2** you learned to identify "just the facts."

In **STEP 3** you learned that your feelings result from your needs being met, or not met, and are never the result of what another person does or doesn't do.

In steps four through seven you practiced new ways of relating to yourself.

In **STEP 4** you took ownership of your thinking and focused your attention on your feelings and needs.

In **STEP 5** you experienced a fuller sense of self because you got in touch with your needs and realized that you can take positive action in meeting those needs.

In **STEP 6** and **7**, you began to envision *positive actions* that are in harmony with meeting your needs *right now*.

In steps eight through ten you practiced new ways of relating to others.

In **STEP 8** you refocused your awareness on the others involved, connected with their feelings and needs, and identified actions that might contribute to meeting their needs.

In **STEP 9** you chose who you would like to speak first, knowing that you can continue the dialog until everyone's needs are met through actions everyone is willing to take.

In **STEP 10**, you finally put it all together and began a dance of communication, where you took turns expressing how you felt and receiving how the other person felt. You stayed focused on making clear requests and tuned in to how you felt about what is being requested of you. You continued to dance until everyone's needs were met through actions everyone agreed to take.

Summing Up

Every minute, every one of us is alive with needs and values seeking expression. You love to live in harmony with your values, and you love to contribute to others' experience of harmony, when you can do so with no element of coercion involved. Moment by moment, with honesty and empathy, you can meet your needs, and bring your values to life. By practicing these 10 Steps you truly can transform anger into compassionate connections.

Now Go Practice

On the following pages you will find Practice Pages you can use to write down a situation where you will practice these new ways of understanding and relating to your feelings of anger, of relating to yourself and relating to others.

Use each page as a guide to gaining the clarity you need and then move on to the next step. Use this opportunity to reframe your understanding of what happened: Identify your feelings, needs, actions you can take to have these needs met, and clear, doable requests you can make of yourself and others to create truly satisfying relationships. When you have completed filling out all ten Practice Pages, take action! It's never too late to clean up a messy situation. You can have the compassionate connection you want—even now.

Use each of these pages as a guide to:

- the clarity you need to understand what happened during an angry conflict
- identify your feelings and needs
- identify actions you can take to have these needs met
- formulate clear, doable requests you can make of yourself and others
- create truly satisfying relationships

STEP 1—Your Anger-Warning Signal

Your anger-warning signal is telling you to "stop and look under your emotional hood." Write down your most "angry thought" and then identify an outcome that would make life more satisfying for everyone.

_____

_____

_____

_____

_____

_____

STEP 2—Just the Facts

Identify "just the facts." Take a clear look at what you are reacting to and write down a clear observation of the situation itself. Write down these facts, making sure not to mix in your judgments.

_____

_____

_____

_____

_____

_____

STEP 3—Take Responsibility

Identify your feelings that result from your needs not being met and write these feelings down. Remember your feelings are never the result of what another person does or doesn't do.

_____

_____

_____

_____

_____

_____

STEP 4—Name the Blame

Take ownership of your thinking and focus your attention on the needs you have that, if they were met, would create an outcome that would make life more satisfying for everyone. Write down which unmet needs are causing your thinking.

_____

_____

_____

_____

_____

STEP 5—Determine "Your" Needs

Now get in touch with your needs and how these generate your feelings. Write down how you feel now that you realize that you can take positive action in meeting those needs.

_____

_____

_____

_____

_____

STEP 6—The "Do" Behind the "Don't"

Identify any actions you want taken and write down those that are expressed in the negative as "stop," "don't," "quit," etc. and translate these into positive actions that are in harmony with meeting your needs right now.

STEP 7—Clear Action Requests

Focus on the power you and others have—the power to deliberately make life more wonderful through the use of a "present tense" request. Write these down.

STEP 8—Name Their Feelings and Needs

Now that you are clear, refocus your awareness on the others involved, connect with their feelings and needs, and identified actions that might contribute to meeting their needs. Write these down.

_____

_____

_____

_____

_____

_____

STEP 9—Who Goes First?

Here is where you get to chose whose needs come first, commit to continuing the dialog until everyone's needs are met through actions everyone is willing to take. Write down how you will start the conversation with the others involved.

_____

_____

_____

_____

_____

_____

STEP 10—Now Start Talking

Imagine how you will be when you begin this dance of communication. How will you stay focused on making clear requests and tuned in to how you feel about what is being requested of you? Write down a strategy that will support you in continuing the communication dance until everyone's needs are met.

_____

_____

_____

_____

_____

_____

_____

How You Can Use the NVC Process

| Clearly expressing
how **I am**
without blaming
or criticizing | Empathically receiving
how **you are**
without hearing
blame or criticism |

OBSERVATIONS

1. What I observe *(see, hear, remember, imagine, free from my evaluations)* that does or does not contribute to my well-being:

   "When I (see, hear) . . . "

1. What you observe *(see, hear, remember, imagine, free from your evaluations)* that does or does not contribute to your well-being:

   "When you see/hear . . . "

   (Sometimes unspoken when offering empathy)

FEELINGS

2. How I feel *(emotion or sensation rather than thought)* in relation to what I observe:

   "I feel . . . "

2. How you feel *(emotion or sensation rather than thought)* in relation to what you observe:

   "You feel . . ."

NEEDS

3. What I need or value *(rather than a preference, or a specific action)* that causes my feelings:

   " . . . because I need/value . . . "

3. What you need or value *(rather than a preference, or a specific action)* that causes your feelings:

   " . . . because you need/value . . ."

| Clearly requesting that
which would enrich **my**
life without demanding | Empathically receiving that
which would enrich **your** life
without hearing any demand |

REQUESTS

4. The concrete actions I would like taken:

   "Would you be willing to . . . ?"

4. The concrete actions you would like taken:

   "Would you like . . . ?"

   (Sometimes unspoken when offering empathy)

Some Basic Feelings We All Have

Feelings when needs are fulfilled

- Amazed
- Comfortable
- Confident
- Eager
- Energetic
- Fulfilled
- Glad
- Hopeful
- Inspired
- Intrigued
- Joyous
- Moved
- Optimistic
- Proud
- Relieved
- Stimulated
- Surprised
- Thankful
- Touched
- Trustful

Feelings when needs are not fulfilled

- Angry
- Annoyed
- Concerned
- Confused
- Disappointed
- Discouraged
- Distressed
- Embarrassed
- Frustrated
- Helpless
- Hopeless
- Impatient
- Irritated
- Lonely
- Nervous
- Overwhelmed
- Puzzled
- Reluctant
- Sad
- Uncomfortable

Some Basic Needs We All Have

Autonomy
- Choosing dreams/goals/values
- Choosing plans for fulfilling one's dreams, goals, values

Celebration
- Celebrating the creation of life and dreams fulfilled
- Celebrating losses: loved ones, dreams, etc. (mourning)

Integrity
- Authenticity • Creativity
- Meaning • Self-worth

Interdependence
- Acceptance • Appreciation
- Closeness • Community
- Consideration
- Contribution to the enrichment of life
- Emotional Safety • Empathy

Physical Nurturance
- Air • Food
- Movement, exercise
- Protection from life-threatening forms of life: viruses, bacteria, insects, predatory animals
- Rest • Sexual expression
- Shelter • Touch • Water

Play
- Fun • Laughter

Spiritual Communion
- Beauty • Harmony
- Inspiration • Order • Peace

- Honesty (the empowering honesty that enables us to learn from our limitations)
- Love • Reassurance
- Respect • Support
- Trust • Understanding

About PuddleDancer Press

PuddleDancer Press (PDP) is the premier publisher of Nonviolent Communication™-related works. Its mission is to provide high-quality materials that help people create a world in which all needs are met compassionately. PDP is the unofficial marketing arm of the international Center for Nonviolent Communication. Publishing revenues are used to develop and implement NVC promotion, educational materials, and media campaigns. By working in partnership with CNVC and NVC trainers, teams, and local supporters, PDP has created a comprehensive, cost-effective promotion effort that has helped bring NVC to thousands more people each year.

Since 2003, PDP has donated over 50,000 NVC books to organizations, decision-makers, and individuals in need around the world. This program is supported in part by donations to CNVC and by partnerships with like-minded organizations around the world. To ensure the continuation of this program, please make a tax-deductible donation to CNVC earmarked to the Book Giveaway Campaign, at www.CNVC.org/donation

Visit the PDP website at www.NonviolentCommunication.com to find the following resources:

- **Shop NVC**—Continue your learning. Purchase our NVC titles online safely and conveniently. Find multiple-copy and package discounts, learn more about our authors, and read dozens of book endorsements from renowned leaders, educators, relationship experts, and more.

- **NVC Quick Connect e-Newsletter**—Sign up today to receive our monthly e-Newsletter, filled with expert articles, resources, related news, and exclusive specials on NVC learning materials. Archived e-Newsletters are also available.

- **Help Share NVC**—Access hundreds of valuable tools, resources, and adaptable documents to help you share NVC, form a local NVC community, coordinate NVC workshops and trainings, and promote the life-enriching benefits of NVC training to organizations and communities in your area. Sign up for our NVC Promotion e-Bulletin to get all the latest tips and tools.

- **For the Press**—Journalists and producers can access author bios and photos, recently published articles in the media, video clips, and other valuable information.

- **About NVC**—Learn more about these life-changing communication skills including an overview of the four-part process, Key Facts about NVC, benefits of the NVC process, and access to our NVC e-Newsletter and Article Archives.

For more information, please contact PuddleDancer Press at:

P.O. Box 231129 • Encinitas CA 92024
Phone: 858-759-6963 • Fax: 858-759-6967
Email: email@puddledancer.com • www.NonviolentCommunication.com

About CNVC and NVC

About CNVC

Founded in 1984 by Dr. Marshall B. Rosenberg, the Center for Nonviolent Communication (CNVC) is an international nonprofit peacemaking organization whose vision is a world where everyone's needs are met peacefully. CNVC is devoted to supporting the spread of Nonviolent Communication (NVC) around the world.

NVC is now being taught around the globe in communities, schools, prisons, mediation centers, churches, businesses, professional conferences, and more. Dr. Rosenberg spends more than 250 days each year teaching NVC in some of the most impoverished, war-torn states of the world. More than 200 certified trainers and hundreds more teach NVC to approximately 250,000 people each year in thirty-five countries.

CNVC believes that NVC training is a crucial step to continue building a compassionate, peaceful society. Your tax-deductible donation will help CNVC continue to provide training in some of the most impoverished, violent corners of the world. It will also support the development and continuation of organized projects aimed at bringing NVC training to high-need geographic regions and populations.

CNVC provides many valuable resources to support the continued growth of NVC worldwide. To make a tax-deductible donation or to learn more about the resources available, visit their website at www.CNVC.org.

For more information, please contact CNVC at:

5600 San Francisco Rd. NE Suite A, Albuquerque, NM 87109
Ph: 505-244-4041 • Fax: 505-247-0414
Email: cnvc@CNVC.org • Website: www.CNVC.org

About NVC

From the bedroom to the boardroom, from the classroom to the war zone, Nonviolent Communication (NVC) is changing lives every day. NVC provides an easy-to-grasp, effective method to get to the root of violence and pain peacefully. By examining the unmet needs behind what we do and say, NVC helps reduce hostility, heal pain, and strengthen professional and personal relationships.

NVC helps us reach beneath the surface and discover what is alive and vital within us, and how all of our actions are based on human needs that we are seeking to meet. We learn to develop a vocabulary of feelings and needs that helps us more clearly express what is going on in us at any given moment. When we understand and acknowledge our needs, we develop a shared foundation for much more satisfying relationships. Join the thousands of people worldwide who have improved their relationships and their lives with this simple yet revolutionary process.

Nonviolent Communication:
A Language of Life, Second Edition

Create Your Life, Your Relationships, and Your World
in Harmony with Your Values

Marshall B. Rosenberg, Ph.D.

$17.95 — Trade Paper 6x9, 240pp
ISBN: 978-1-892005-03-8

In this internationally acclaimed text, Marshall Rosenberg offers insightful stories, anecdotes, practical exercises and role-plays that will literally change your approach to communication for the better. Nonviolent Communication partners practical skills with a powerful consciousness to help us get what we want peacefully.

Discover how the language you use can strengthen your relationships, build trust, prevent or resolve conflicts peacefully, and heal pain. Over 400,000 copies of this landmark text have been sold in 20 languages around the globe.

"Nonviolent communication is a simple yet powerful methodology for communicating in a way that meets both parties' needs. This is one of the most useful books you will ever read."
　　　　　—William Ury, co-author of *Getting to Yes* and author of *The Third Side*

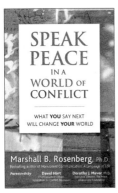

Speak Peace in a World of Conflict

What You Say Next Will Change Your World

by Marshall B. Rosenberg, Ph.D.

$15.95 — Trade Paper 5-3/8x8-3/8, 240pp
ISBN: 978-1-892005-17-5

International peacemaker, mediator, and healer, Rosenberg shows you how the language you use is the key to enriching life. *Speak Peace* is filled with inspiring stories, lessons, and ideas drawn from over 40 years of mediating conflicts and healing relationships in some of the most war-torn, impoverished, and violent corners of the world. Find insight, practical skills, and powerful tools that will profoundly change your relationships and the course of your life for the better.

Discover how you can create an internal consciousness of peace as the first step toward effective personal, professional, and social change. Find complete chapters on the mechanics of Speaking Peace, conflict resolution, transforming business culture, transforming enemy images, addressing terrorism, transforming authoritarian structures, expressing and receiving gratitude, and social change.

Bestselling author of the internationally acclaimed,
Nonviolent Communication: A Language of Life

Available from PDP, CNVC, all major bookstores, and Amazon.com
Distributed by IPG: 800-888-4741

Trade Booklets from PuddleDancer Press

Being Me, Loving You • *A Practical Guide to Extraordinary Relationships* **by Marshall B. Rosenberg, Ph.D.** • Watch your relationships strengthen as you learn to think of love as something you "do," something you give freely from the heart. 80pp, ISBN: 978-1-892005-16-8 • **$6.95**

Getting Past the Pain Between Us • *Healing and Reconciliation Without Compromise* **by Marshall B. Rosenberg, Ph.D.** • Learn simple steps to create the heartfelt presence necessary for lasting healing to occur—great for mediators, counselors, families, and couples. 48pp, ISBN: 978-1-892005-07-6 • **$6.95**

The Heart of Social Change • *How to Make a Difference in Your World* **by Marshall B. Rosenberg, Ph.D.** • Learn how creating an internal consciousness of compassion can impact your social change efforts. 48pp, ISBN: 978-1-892005-10-6 • **$6.95**

Parenting from Your Heart • *Sharing the Gifts of Compassion, Connection, and Choice* **by Inbal Kashtan** • Filled with insight and practical skills, this booklet will help you transform your parenting to address every day challenges. 48pp, ISBN: 978-1-892005-08-3 • **$6.95**

Practical Spirituality • *Reflections on the Spiritual Basis of Nonviolent Communication* **by Marshall B. Rosenberg, Ph.D.** • Marshall's views on the spiritual origins and underpinnings of NVC, and how practicing the process helps him connect to the Divine. 48pp, ISBN: 978-1-892005-14-4 • **$6.95**

Raising Children Compassionately • *Parenting the Nonviolent Communication Way* **by Marshall B. Rosenberg, Ph.D.** • Learn to create a mutually respectful, enriching family dynamic filled with heartfelt communication. 32pp, ISBN: 978-1-892005-09-0 • **$5.95**

The Surprising Purpose of Anger • *Beyond Anger Management: Finding the Gift* **by Marshall B. Rosenberg, Ph.D.** • Rosenberg shows you how to use anger to discover what you need, and then how to meet your needs in more constructive, healthy ways. 48pp, ISBN: 978-1-892005-15-1 • **$6.95**

Teaching Children Compassionately • *How Students and Teachers Can Succeed with Mutual Understanding* **by Marshall B. Rosenberg, Ph.D.** • In this national keynote address to Montessori educators, Rosenberg describes his progressive, radical approach to teaching that centers on compassionate connection. 48pp, ISBN: 978-1-892005-11-3 • **$6.95**

We Can Work It Out • *Resolving Conflicts Peacefully and Powerfully* **by Marshall B. Rosenberg, Ph.D.** • Practical suggestions for fostering empathic connection, genuine cooperation, and satisfying resolutions in even the most difficult situations. 32pp, ISBN: 978-1-892005-12-0 • **$5.95**

What's Making You Angry? • *10 Steps to Transforming Anger So Everyone Wins* **by Shari Klein and Neill Gibson** • A powerful, step-by-step approach to transform anger to find healthy, mutually satisfying outcomes. 32pp, ISBN: 978-1-892005-13-7 • **$5.95**

Available from PDP, CNVC, all major bookstores, and Amazon.com. Distributed by IPG: 800-888-4741. For more information about these booklets or to order online visit www.NonviolentCommunication.com